VIDEO ACCESS INCLUDED

PROGRESSIVE ROCK
RHYTHM GUITAR

BY TRAVIS LEVRIER

To access video visit:
www.halleonard.com/mylibrary

Enter Code
2456-7944-9838-0264

Cover photo: © Chantelle Renee Photography

ISBN 978-1-4950-4579-0

7777 W. BLUEMOUND RD. P.O. BOX 13819 MILWAUKEE, WI 53213

In Australia Contact:
Hal Leonard Australia Pty. Ltd.
4 Lentara Court
Cheltenham, Victoria, 3192 Australia
Email: ausadmin@halleonard.com.au

Visit Hal Leonard Online at
www.halleonard.com

TABLE OF CONTENTS

INTRODUCTION

Welcome to *Progressive Rock Rhythm Guitar*! This book is based on skills and techniques I've picked up across the last decade in which I've been a full-time touring guitarist, primarily playing rhythm guitar. I've carefully crafted the riffs and examples in this course to serve as multi-faceted examples outlining the fundamentals of technical, tonal, and rhythmic approaches to the guitar in an applied setting.

There's a limitless supply of books regarding lead guitar and solos, but I realized that there's not much material focused on rhythm guitar, and especially not with a specific focus on its role within the context of prog music. My aim with this book is to bring something new to the table, providing you with the material and hands-on experience to help you take your rhythm guitar playing to the next level. This book is designed for the intermediate guitarist who is looking to gain a better understanding of playing in common odd time signatures.

The examples in *Progressive Rock Rhythm Guitar* encompass a wide variety of styles and mobilize a wide array of guitar techniques, specifically designed to push your abilities as a rhythm guitarist. The goal is not only to teach you prog guitar riffs, but to help increase awareness and understanding of your role within a band setting, playing along with accompaniments from my very own rhythm section in Scale the Summit (Mark Michell and J.C. Bryant).

Whether I'm teaching one-on-one or performing a clinic, my aim is to inspire my students and help kindle their passion. This was the primary inspiration behind *Progressive Rock Rhythm Guitar*, and I hope it helps you to gain fresh perspective on your instrument.

Thanks.

—Travis

ABOUT THE AUTHOR

Travis LeVrier is a guitarist, clinician, and educator, known primarily for his work in guitar-driven instrumental band, Scale the Summit, dubbed "essential prog" by *Guitar World* magazine. LeVrier first picked up the guitar at age 14, quickly developing a taste for prog music. His passion drove him to further his education at Hollywood's Musicians Institute, where he founded STS, thus beginning a decade-long career as a touring musician. Since 2004, he has recorded five albums and taken part in dozens of tours, sharing the stage with prog heavy-hitters such as Yes, Dream Theater, Zappa Plays Zappa, Between the Buried and Me, Periphery, and Protest the Hero. Travis is currently holding down guitar duties for technical death metal outfit, Entheos. When he's not on the road, you'll find him teaching guitar lessons in his studio in Houston, TX.

CHAPTER 1
4/4 TIME

EXAMPLE 1

In this first example, we're going to take a look at how you can take a simple two-chord progression in a 4/4 time signature and make it more progressive by using interesting chords and rhythms. This riff is in the key of E minor and uses the chords Em9 and Bm11. Each measure starts with syncopated strums of the entire chord, followed by an arpeggiated picking pattern of two muted 16th notes and four eighth notes that are allowed to ring out. Goal tempo is 120 bpm.

EXAMPLE 2

This next one is a happy, upbeat riff in 4/4 time. It's a two-part riff based around the three-note add9 and maj7th chord shapes in two different positions on the low E, A, and D strings. The A section of the riff is completely single-note based and made up entirely of quarter notes and eighth notes. Although it may sound like an easy riff, the picking can be surprisingly trouble-some if you're not careful. The B section is more chord-based, with single notes played on the low E string in-between the full chord strums. Goal tempo is 180 bpm.

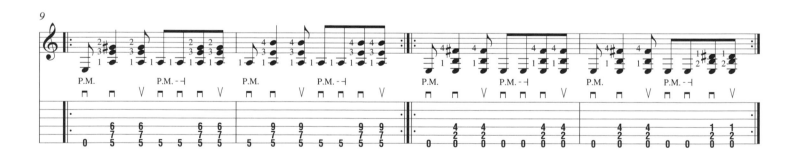

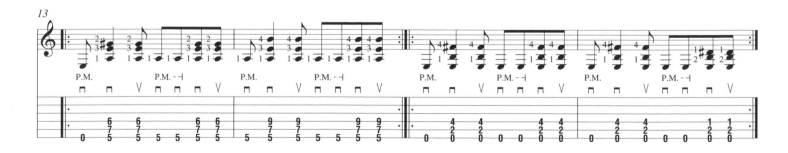

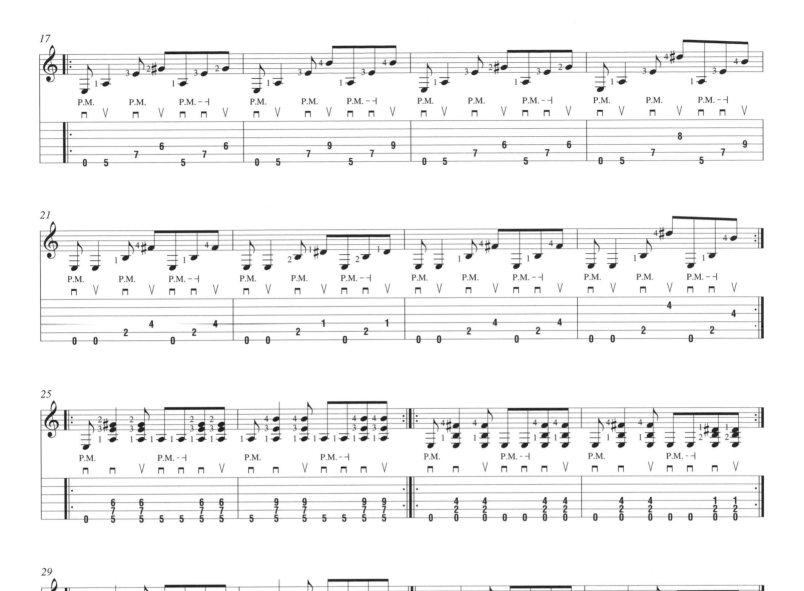

EXAMPLE 3

In this example, we'll be using the chords Bsus4/E and Bmaj7sus4/E. Both chord voicings are easy to play and have a very big sound due to the open low E and B strings. The riff has a good mixture of eighth notes, 16th notes, and dotted eighth notes in a 4/4 time signature, with the last strum in each measure ringing out over the bar line and into the following measure. The picking pattern for this example is pretty straightforward, but there are a couple of instances where you will accent the chord hits with an upstroke. Goal tempo is 130 beats per minute (bpm).

EXAMPLE 4

In this next example, we'll be using a series of chords that include the open high E and B strings. Most of these chord shapes are non-traditional; hopefully, they'll become new options for you when choosing chords to play. The riff is in 4/4 time and has a rhythm of straight eighth notes plus one short 16th-note gallop thrown in. You'll be using the open B and E strings at the end of each pattern for an almost harp-like sound that rings out nicely. Goal tempo is 140 bpm.

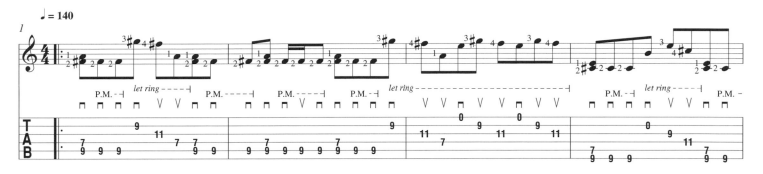

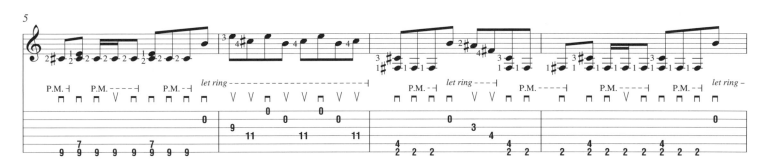

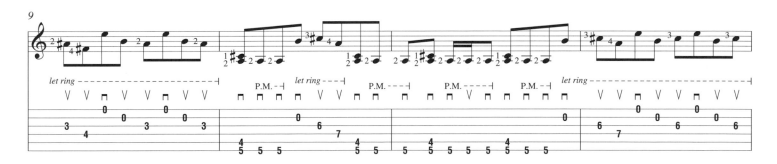

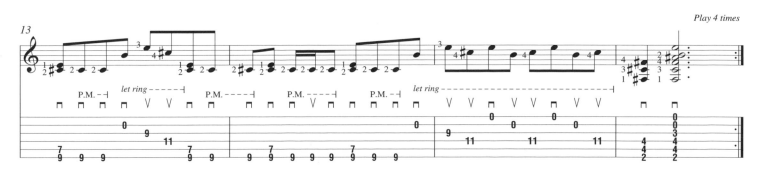

EXAMPLE 5

In this next example, we'll look at some chords in the key of B major and how we can link them together by using single-note gallop patterns, as well as arpeggiating certain parts of the chords to produce a more complete-sounding riff. It starts off with a Badd9 chord, then moves on to Bsus2, Bmaj7, and, finally, G#m7. Practice the chord changes before trying to play the entire sequence. This riff also focuses on pick control, combining both alternate picking and economy (sweep) picking. Goal tempo is 130 bpm.

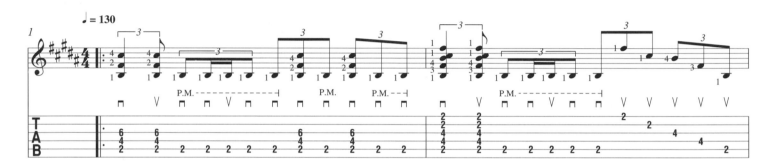

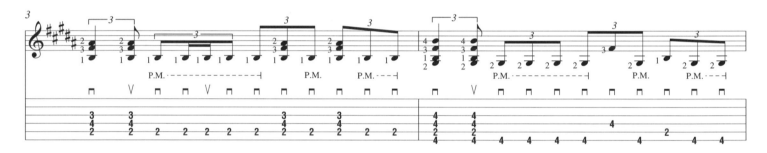

CHAPTER 2
TRIPLETS

EXAMPLE 1

This example is in 4/4 time and uses the chords Bsus2/add♯4 and Gsus2/add♯4. It's made up entirely of eighth-note triplets, but the way we break up the full chord strums and the single notes on the low E string gives it an interesting rhythm pattern. Study the suggested picking pattern, as there are parts in the second and fourth measures that you'll want to accent with upstrokes. Goal tempo is 130 bpm.

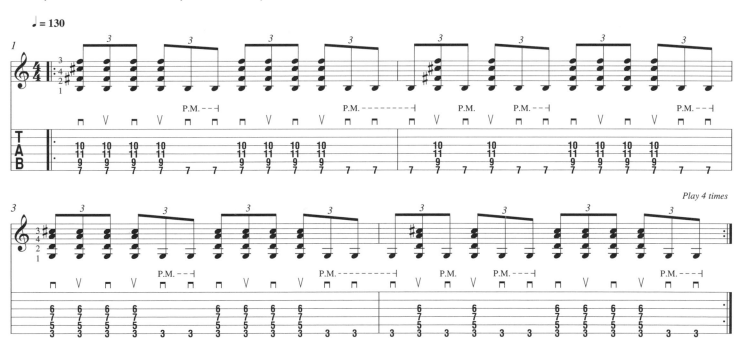

EXAMPLE 2

This next riff is another two-part example. Section A is a palm-muted single-note pattern arpeggiating Gadd9, Aadd9, and Eadd9 chords on the low E, A, and D strings. The picking pattern is down-down-up for the entire part. Section B follows those same chord changes but is now played with a strummed rhythm; consequently, the picking pattern changes to mostly alternate strumming, with a pair of palm-muted downstrokes in a few spots. Goal tempo is 130 bpm.

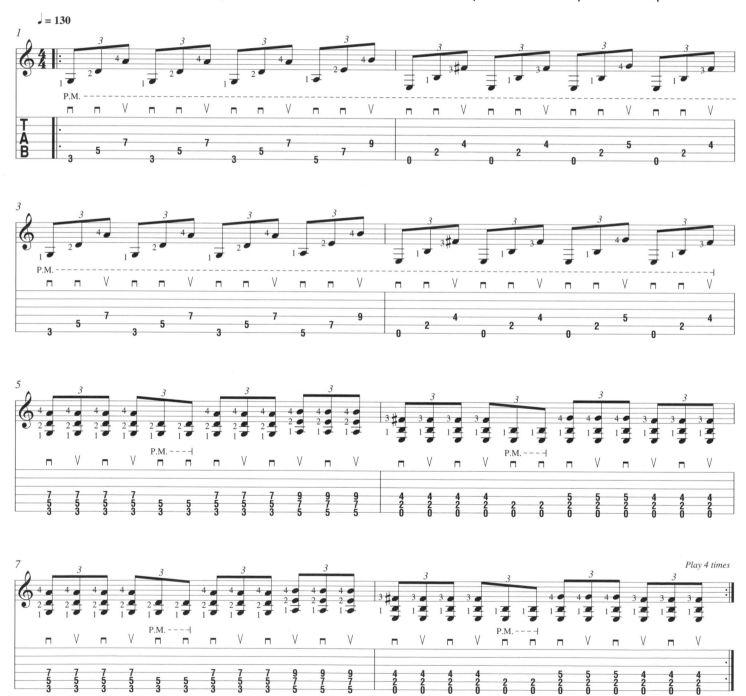

EXAMPLE 3

This next riff uses the exact same rhythm as the previous one, but we'll pair it with an entirely different set of chords, giving it a completely different sound. Practice the chord changes individually before you try them with the rhythm pattern. Goal tempo is 120 bpm.

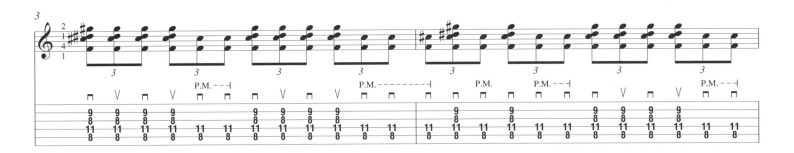

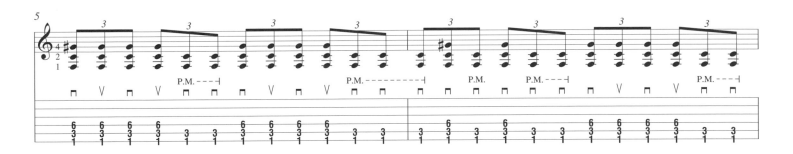

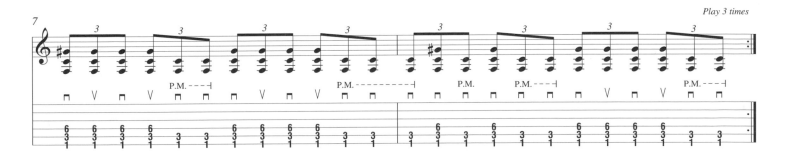

EXAMPLE 4

This next example is based on the A Lydian mode. It's a single-note riff played primarily with eighth-note triplets. The first two measures pair the open low-E string with notes from the A Lydian mode on the A string. The last two measures omit the open low-E string in favor of fretted notes of the A Lydian mode. Goal tempo is 135 bpm.

EXAMPLE 5

This next riff is meant to be played over the previous one to create a two-guitar-part layer. It's also a single-note riff based on the A Lydian mode and primarily played with eighth-note triplets. Once you've learned both parts, you could record one and play the other part over it, or get together with a guitar-playing buddy and jam over it. Goal tempo is 135 bpm.

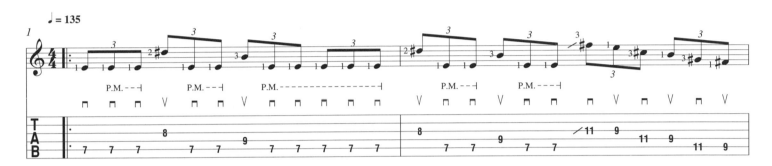

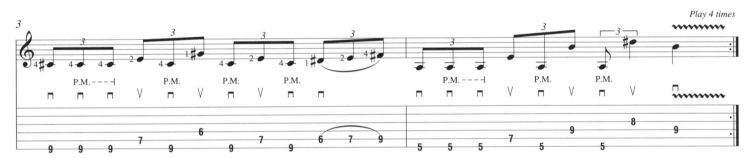

EXAMPLE 6

This next riff continues our triplet studies. There are two main sections: for the A section, we'll be playing a single-note pattern in an eighth-note triplet rhythm; for the B section, we'll still be playing eighth-note triplets, but this time, full chord strums are used. Be sure to work on muting all of the strings during the rests in this section. Goal Tempo: 140 bpm.

♩ = 140

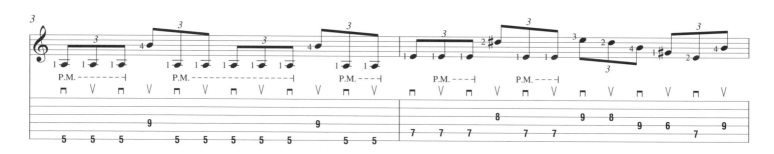

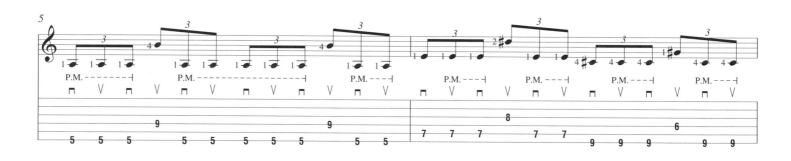

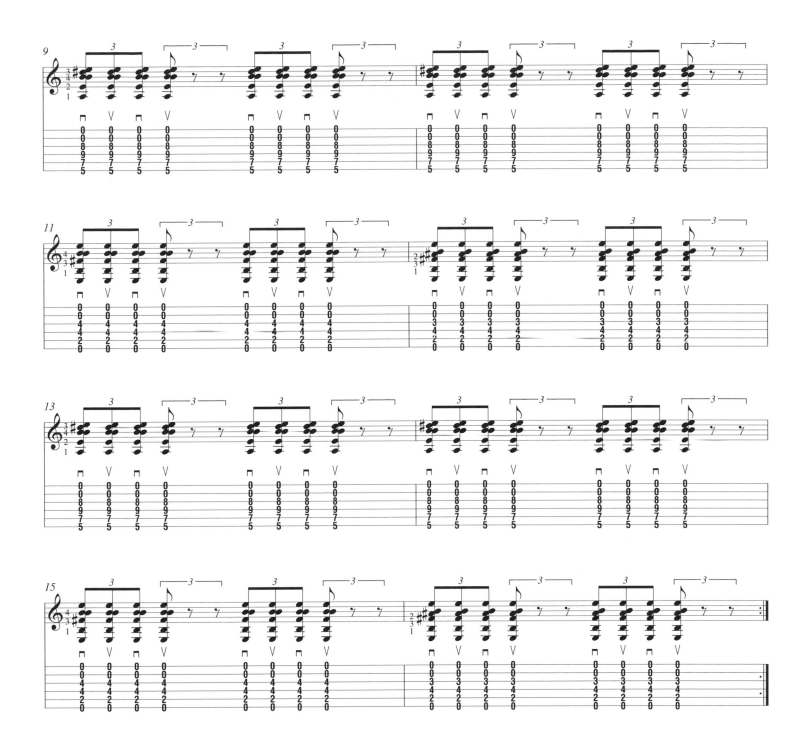

EXAMPLE 7

This next example is a single-note riff that uses eighth-note triplets and incorporates quite a bit of string skipping throughout. After a short intro, two main parts are alternated. Use strict alternate picking for these two parts, but since there is so much string skipping, it's probably going to feel a little awkward at first. Therefore, be sure to start off slowly so you can focus on picking accuracy and finger movement from string to string. Goal tempo is 130 bpm.

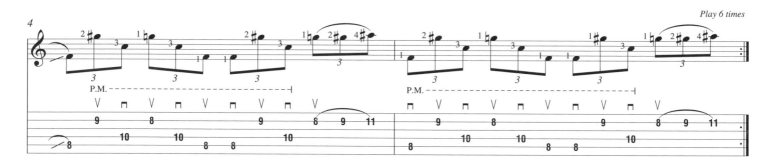

CHAPTER 3
5/4 AND 5/8 TIME

EXAMPLE 1

For this first example in 5/4 time, we're going to start with two strums of a really cool, huge-sounding chord, Bmaj7sus4/E. Rhythmically, each strum is equivalent to a dotted eighth note. Don't let that chord name scare you, because it's a very easy chord to play. After the initial two dotted eighth-note strums, we'll move up to play a group of six palm-muted 16th notes on the open low-E string, and then repeat that entire pattern once more. Following the repetition of that pattern, we'll go into a single strum of a C#min7♭13 chord played in fourth position. That chord will ring out as a dotted half note, followed by two arpeggiated single notes to end the measure. The pattern is then restated. Goal tempo is 120 bpm.

EXAMPLE 2

This next riff, also played in 5/4, consists entirely of straight eighth notes but is a bit of a finger-twister in a couple of sections. In the first two measures, we're playing a C major seventh arpeggio pattern. Take note of the picking pattern that is notated, as it's not entirely straight alternate picking. In the next two measures, we're playing a pattern of notes from the A minor scale in fifth position. Examine the suggested fingering for each section, and notice that the picking pattern changes to straight alternate picking for the last two measures. Goal tempo is 160 bpm.

EXAMPLE 3

This next example in 5/4 is in the key of A major. The chords used are as follows: F#m11, C#m7#5, F#m9, Amaj9, and Emaj9. The riff has a nice mixture of hammer-ons and slides to transition from one chord to the next. Also included within each chord change is an arpeggiated picking pattern, which should be allowed to let ring out. Goal Tempo: 120 bpm.

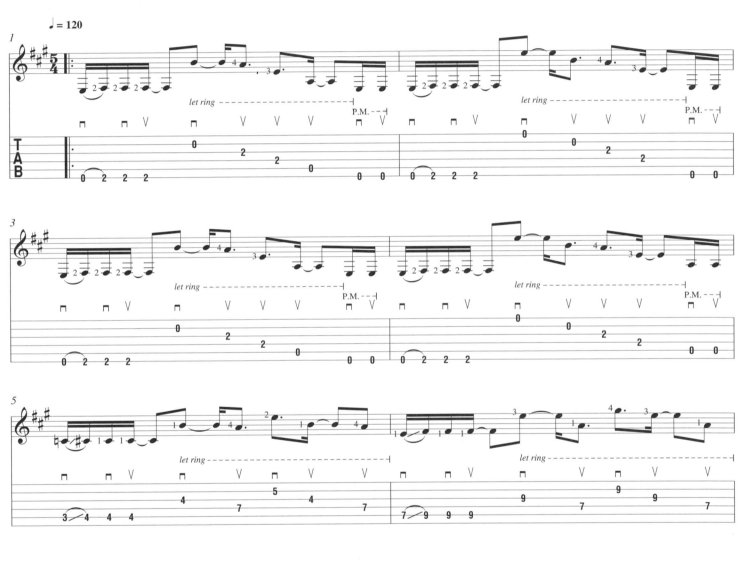

EXAMPLE 4

For this next riff, we'll be arpeggiating a single-note pattern in 5/4. We'll start with a C#m9 chord in seventh position. I wanted to break up the notes slightly, so I started with a 2–2–1 pattern and then immediately followed it with a 2–1–2 pattern just to mix it up a bit. Rhythmically, this riff is not hard, but the combination of these two patterns, back to back, can be a little tricky at first. Be sure to spend some time practicing it on just one chord before you work through the entire progression. Goal Tempo: 160 bpm.

EXAMPLE 5

In this next riff, we'll be using dotted eighth notes for most of the rhythm, with a couple spots that feature 16th notes, as well. The first measure, which is in 5/4, begins with an Emaj9 chord played in seventh position. We'll start by alternating between the chord and the open low-E string, and then arpeggiate three notes before ending the measure with two 16th-note palm mutes. The second measure is in 8/4 and uses an Aadd9 voicing that features the major 3rd on the G string, played with your second finger. We'll start this measure by alternating between strumming all six strings, and then just the bottom three. The rest of the measure is pretty easy to follow. Practice switching between these two chord shapes before you try the entire riff. Goal tempo is 120 bpm.

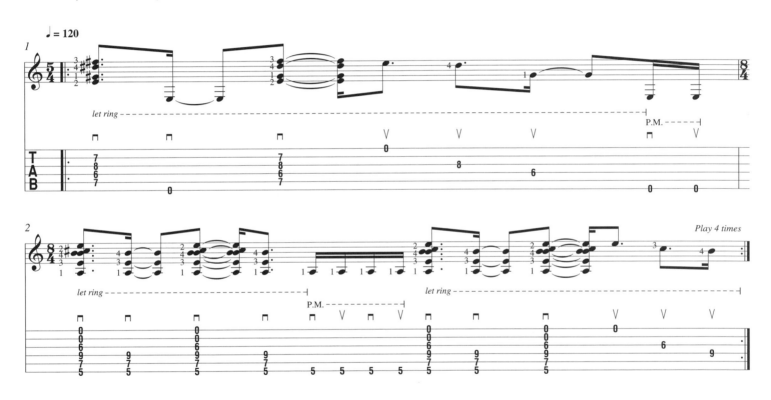

EXAMPLE 6

In this next example in 5/4, we're going to take a look at how you can create a single-note riff that is fairly simple, rhythmically, but make it melodically interesting by progressing through note choices that are all nearby. We'll be using quite a bit of string skipping throughout the entire riff, but the picking pattern is straight alternate picking. Goal tempo is 150 bpm.

EXAMPLE 7

We'll be continuing in 5/4 time in this next example. This riff is a single-note pattern that is based on a B minor ninth arpeggio on the lower three strings. We'll be focusing on our "double picking," going from playing two sets of three notes to two sets of two notes. This should be a great way for you to work on transitioning smoothly from one pattern to the next. Goal Tempo: 180 bpm.

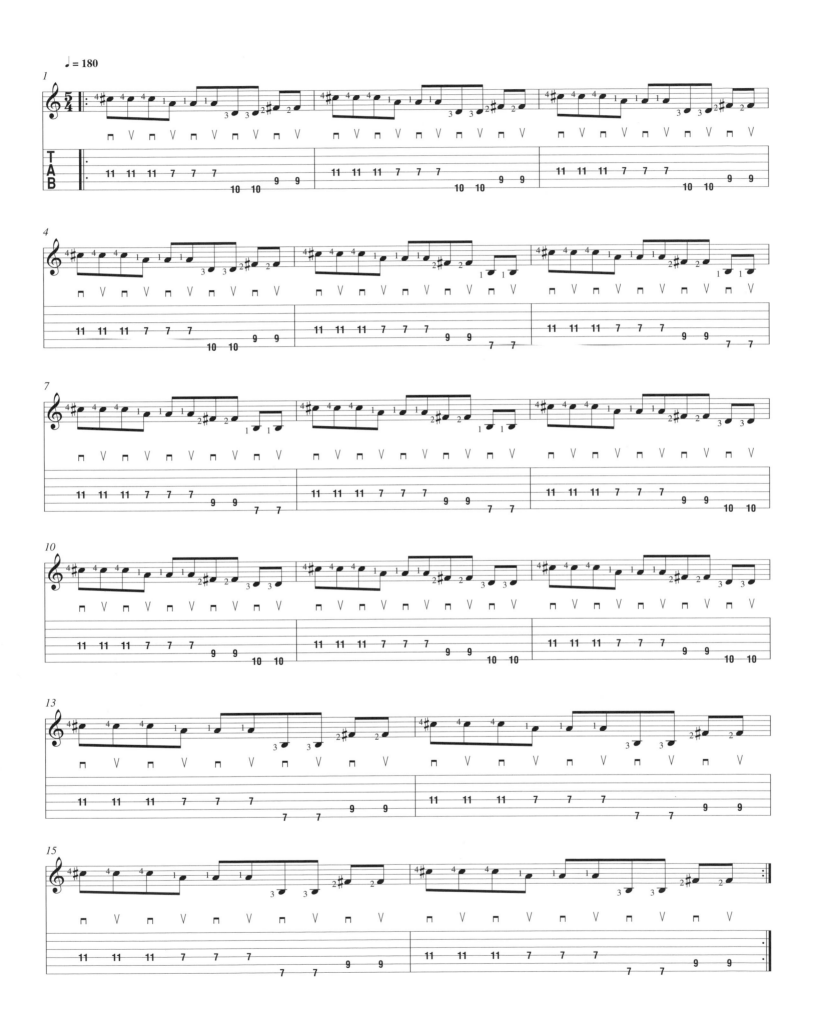

EXAMPLE 8

Let's take a look at yet another commonly used odd time signature, 5/8. In this example, we are once again showcasing how you can create an interesting-sounding arpeggio sequence without having to move all around the fretboard. The initial picking pattern, down-up-down-up-up, is the same for the first two shapes, and then changes to down-up-down-down-up for the last two shapes. Goal tempo is 150 bpm.

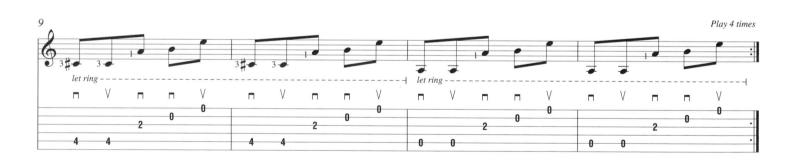

CHAPTER 4
6/4 TIME

EXAMPLE 1

In this example, we'll be taking a look at a riff in 6/4 time, based around two chords, C#m9 and Asus2/add#4. Each chord strum should be accented a little louder than the individual notes played on the low E string in-between strums. This riff will also work on your string-skipping accuracy, as you'll have to quickly jump from the low E string to the high E string to arpeggiate the three notes played on the high E, G, and D strings. The second measure of each chord change is slightly different than the first. The part played on the lower strings is extended, including a quick 16th-note gallop in the middle of the measure. Goal tempo is 160 bpm.

EXAMPLE 2

In this next example, we'll continue along in 6/4 time. All four chord changes in this example are located in the same position on the fretboard. This is a great way to show you that you don't always have to change positions to get the chord that you desire. The chords that we'll be using are: Asus2/add#4, Asus2, C#m11, and Eadd9/G#. Each chord will be played in a rhythm that is equivalent to a dotted quarter note, followed by a five-note gallop pattern on the open A string consisting of two 16th notes, a single eighth note, and then two more 16th notes. Goal tempo is 120 bpm.

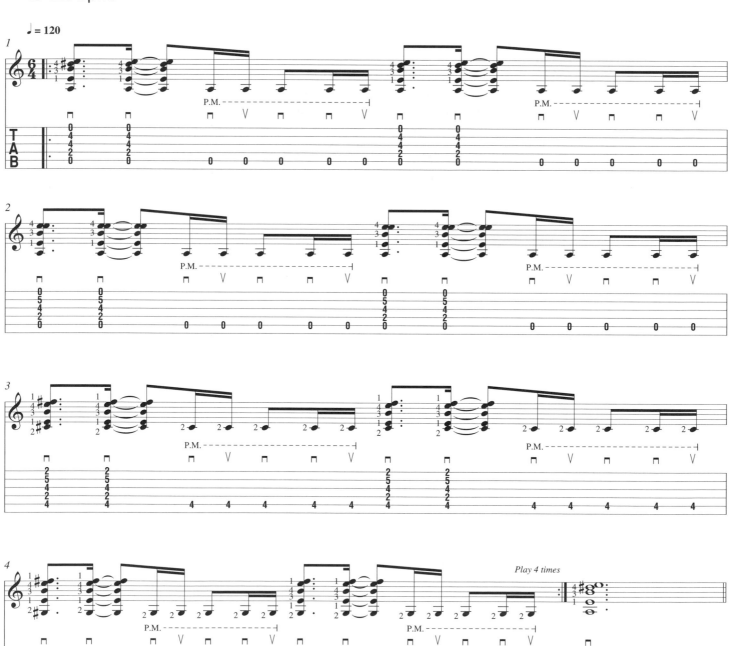

EXAMPLE 3

This next riff in 6/4 is based entirely on the notes of the A Lydian mode. Rhythmically, we'll be playing eighth notes the whole time while arpeggiating a pattern of notes on the lower three strings. The picking pattern is just straight alternate picking, but some string skipping is needed in a few areas. Goal Tempo: 200 bpm.

EXAMPLE 4

For this next example, we'll be taking a look at tapping in odd time and how you can incorporate it into your rhythm playing to create riffs that, without the technique, you could otherwise not play. We'll be playing in a 6/4 time signature, but this example is not complicated, rhythmically, as it only consists of straight 16th notes. However, the two-handed tapping technique that we'll be using to play it can be a little tricky at first. We're going to be outlining two add9 chord shapes, and then adding notes to give one of them a minor sound, and the other a major sound. The first shape is E minor and we'll be playing the following intervals from the root note on the 12th fret of the low E string: root, 5th, 2nd/9th, b3rd, b7th, and 4th. The second shape is G major and we'll be playing the following intervals from the root note on the 15th fret of the low E string: root, 5th, 2nd/9th, 3rd, 6th, and 3rd. Muting with your picking hand is going to be very important for this example, so you'll want to start slowly, making sure that you are keeping the excess string noise under control. Goal tempo is 100 bpm.

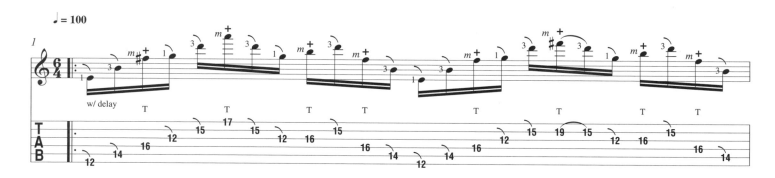

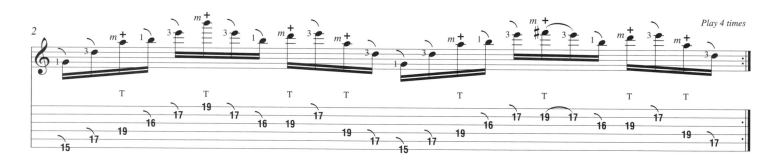

EXAMPLE 5

This next example in 6/4 uses a unique set of chord voicings: F#m11, Amaj9/C#, E6, and Aadd9. This riff has a rhythmic pattern, but it's not played the same on every chord in the progression. We'll also experience a couple of areas where we'll play "over the bar line." Rhythmically, this riff is a combination of quarter notes, eighth notes, and 16th notes. The hardest part will be the chord transitions, so be sure to practice each of those individually before attempting the entire riff. Goal Tempo: 140 bpm.

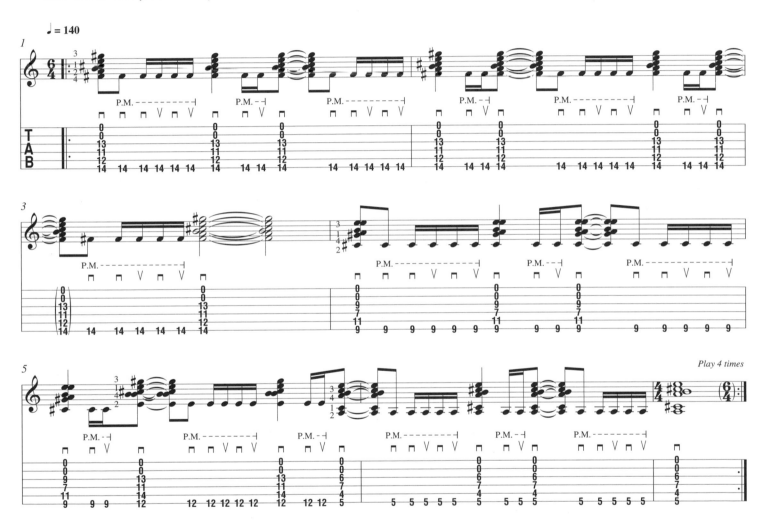

EXAMPLE 6

In this next example, we're going to focus on our picking accuracy when arpeggiating a chord progression. We're still in 6/4 time, this time using the chords Cmaj9#11 and Aadd9/#11. The first measure of each chord is pretty straightforward: you'll arpeggiate four eighth notes, followed by a single strum of the chord, which you'll let ring as a whole note. The second measure of each chord is where things will be slightly more difficult. Here, we'll be using more string skipping and we'll also have to switch the fingering on the G and D strings for the last four eighth notes in the pattern. Be sure to examine the picking pattern for this one, and start off slowly. Goal tempo is 150 bpm.

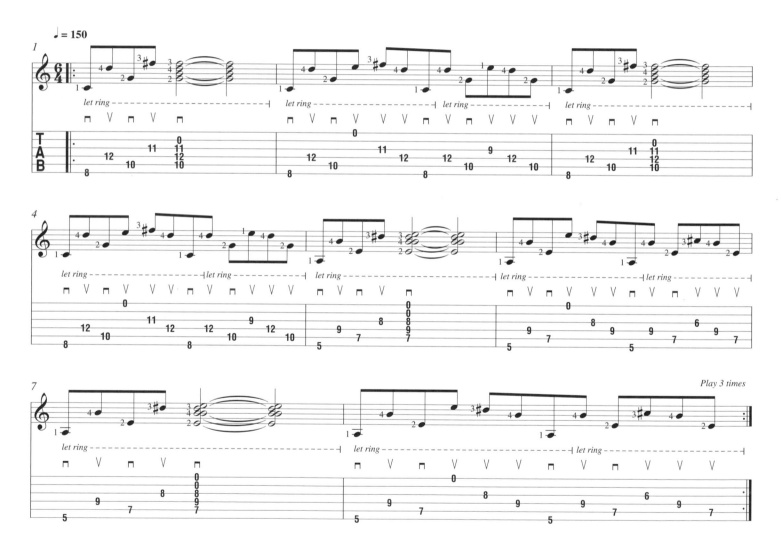

EXAMPLE 7

For our next example in 6/4, we'll be starting off with a simple single-note pattern on the low E and A strings that will be picked with all downstrokes, accenting every note played on the A string. This will be followed by a short bridge of 16th notes before we go into the second section, which will be played the same way as the first section, but is meant to be heavier since we're using full chords now instead of just single notes. The second section will be followed by another bridge of 16th notes, this one setting you up to restart the riff. Goal tempo is 110 bpm.

EXAMPLE 8

Now that we've played a few examples in 6/4 time, let's try to speed things up a bit. For this next one, we're going to start off by going right into a group of six 16th notes that are played on the low E string. That will go directly into a dotted-quarter-note strum of an F#m11 chord played in second position. We'll play that twice in the first measure. After that, we'll go straight into an arpeggiated sequence on the D, G, B, and high E strings. The second repetition of the riff will start off exactly the same but then go into a different arpeggiated sequence (a C#m7#5 chord), followed by the example's ending section. Goal tempo is 160 bpm.

CHAPTER 5
7/4 AND 7/8 TIME

EXAMPLE 1

In this example, we'll be exploring a single-note riff in 7/4 time that uses a pretty straightforward rhythm of all eighth notes. This should be a good way for you to ease into playing in odd time. The riff itself is in the key of C major and uses the same sus2 chord shape in different positions across the fretboard. The picking pattern used for this example is a mixture of a sweep picking and alternate picking. Here it is: down-down-down-up-down-up-up. Remember to palm mute slightly with your picking hand, and keep only one finger on the fretboard at a time versus holding down all three notes of the chord at once. Goal tempo is 180 bpm.

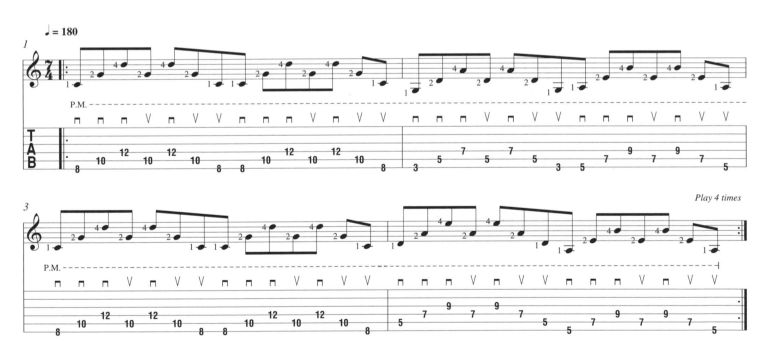

EXAMPLE 2

This next example showcases how you can break up a riff, rhythmically, to get an interesting pattern once you've written a chord progression that you like. We'll start with an Asus2/add#4 chord in second position. The pattern begins with a single quarter-note strum of the entire chord, followed by four palm-muted 16th notes on the open A string. After that, we'll use eighth notes to arpeggiate the top three strings, play four more 16th notes on the open A string, and then end with another arpeggiated pattern. This sequence is then repeated on the remaining chords of the progression. Goal tempo is 140 bpm.

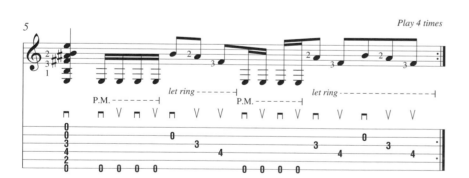

EXAMPLE 3

You'll start this next 7/4 example by strumming an Asus2/add#4 chord with a group of four 16th notes, followed by an eighth-note rest. You'll play that pattern twice and then finish the measure with an arpeggiated single-note "tail" ending. You'll repeat this entire rhythmic pattern in the second measure on another set of chords. Be sure to work on the single-note tail ending in each measure individually, as they are the trickiest part of this example. Goal Tempo: 100 bpm.

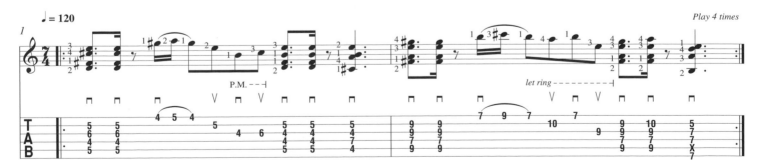

EXAMPLE 4

For this next example in 7/4, we're going to explore some more jazz-style chords: Dmaj9, D6, C#m7#5, F#m9, F#m7, and Bm11. We'll start each measure with syncopated strums of the first chord, followed by a short single-note lick based on that chord. After that, we'll go back to playing syncopated strums, this time on the next group of chords. For the single-note licks in each measure, be sure to use the hammer-ons and pull-offs where notated. Goal tempo is 120 bpm.

EXAMPLE 5

This next riff is a bit tricky. It's in 7/4 time, and while we'll only be using two different chord shapes, we'll be incorporating several other techniques for dynamics, including pick scratches, hammer-ons, and pull-offs. Each measure will start off with a single quarter-note strum of the entire chord. What follows next is a somewhat advanced picking pattern that starts with a few 16th-note palm mutes for a slightly percussive sound and an arpeggiated picking pattern that spans across the rest of the strings. The chords that we'll be using are an F#m11 and an Aadd9 with the major 3rd on the G string. The picking pattern is the hardest part of this riff, so be sure to start slowly and pay close attention to the picking pattern that is notated. Goal tempo is 120 bpm.

EXAMPLE 6

This next example is a tapping riff in 7/4. It's a great way to work on getting both of your hands synced up and working together. Start by hammering on a Dsus2 chord with your fretting hand on the 10th, 12th, and 14th frets of the E, A, and D strings, respectively. We'll then move up to the G string to hammer onto the 10th and 14th frets before tapping a single note on the 21st fret of the same string. You'll then play this same pattern again, except when you get to the G string, you'll change the hammer-on notes to the 10th and 12th frets and tap a single note on the 17th fret. These two patterns are alternated twice.

The final section of the riff moves to hammering onto a Gsus2 chord on the 10th, 12th, and 14th frets of the A, D, and G strings, respectively. This is followed by hammer-ons at the 12th and 14th frets of the G string before tapping a single note on the 19th fret of the same string. This pattern repeats four times before starting the entire riff over. Take a close look at the notation, being aware of the eighth-note rest that occurs after you hammer onto each sus2 chord. Goal Tempo: 155 bpm.

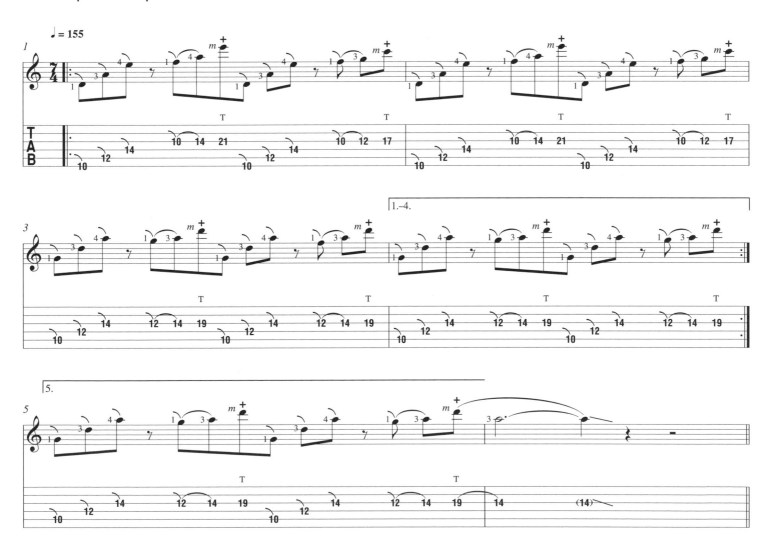

EXAMPLE 7

Here's a riff in 7/8 time that will force you to work on your picking accuracy, hand control, and finger coordination while arpeggiating a chord. We'll be using two different chord shapes, Asus2/add♯4 and Add9, and incorporating a few other techniques in certain areas such as alternate picking, palm muting, and string skipping. Goal tempo is 160 bpm.

CHAPTER 6
3/4, 8/4, AND 9/8 TIME

EXAMPLE 1

In this example, we'll be taking a look at one of the most commonly used odd time signatures in progressive rock, 3/4. We'll be using a few different groups of three notes that span across the high E, B, G, and D strings. Rhythmically, it's not complex, as it's entirely made up of straight eighth notes, so it should be fairly easy to learn. It is, however, a good way to show you how you can create an interesting arpeggiated progression by using only a few notes and changing one or two at a time with notes that are in the same position on the neck. I'm letting each group of three notes ring throughout the entire measure. Goal Tempo: 120 bpm.

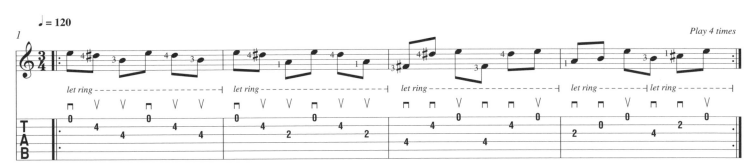

EXAMPLE 2

We'll go for a totally different 3/4 feel in this next example. This is a slower arpeggiated pattern that uses some very lush-sounding chords, all of which incorporate the open B and high-E strings. Make sure to pick/strum each chord clearly, letting them ring out until you transition into the next one. Goal Tempo: 130 bpm.

EXAMPLE 3

This example is a tapping riff in 3/4 that is based around the F minor pentatonic scale. You'll start by hammering onto the eighth and 11th frets of the A string with your first and fourth fingers. Next, you'll use either your first or second finger of your picking hand to tap the 18th fret of the A string (I prefer to use my second finger to tap so I can still hold my pick as usual). After that, a similar pattern is played on the eighth and 10th fret of the D string with your first and third fingers, and you'll again use either your first or second finger of your pick hand to tap, this time onto the 17th fret of the D string. To finish off the pattern, we'll go right back into the first part again, this time adding your third finger to the 10th fret of the A string, making the notes on the eighth and 10th frets 16th notes instead of eighth notes. After you play the entire pattern twice, you'll then move the entire riff down one whole step (two frets). Be sure to use strong hammer-ons with your fretting hand and firm taps with your picking hand. Each note should ring out right up until the next one is played. Goal Tempo: 180 bpm.

EXAMPLE 4

In this next riff, we'll be testing your finger "stretchability" a little bit. We'll be playing two chord voicings in two positions across the bottom four strings of the guitar that will require all four fingers of your fretting hand. Both voicings are based on the three-note sus2 chord shape that is used throughout this book. For the first chord, let's move to eighth position. Using your third finger, you're going to add the ♯4th into this voicing, which is located at the 11th fret of the G string. For the second chord, you'll have to change up the fingering slightly. Using your second finger, you're going to add the major 3rd to the voicing, which is located at the ninth fret of the G string. Now that we've learned the two chord voicings that we'll be using for this riff, let's talk about everything else that is going on. The example is in 8/4 time and will require you to work on your picking accuracy and palm-muting control. We'll also be incorporating the open B and E strings into each of these chords for a very nice, huge sound. Goal Tempo: 100 bpm.

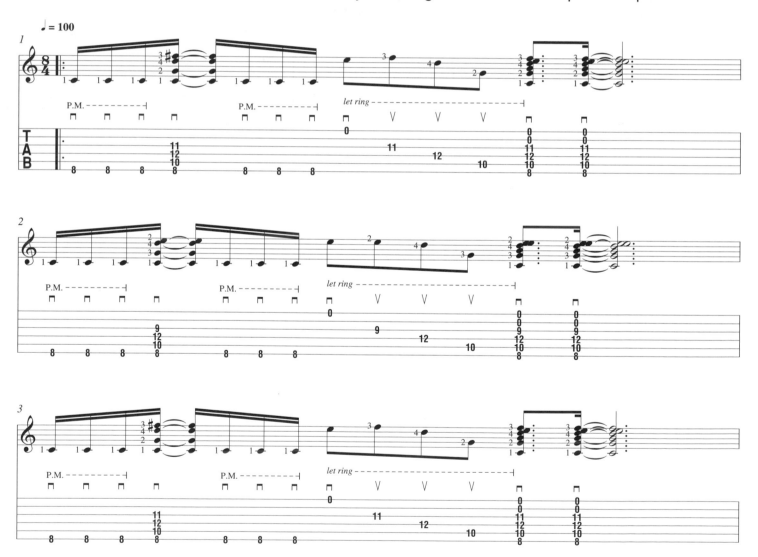

EXAMPLE 5

We're going to continue in 8/4 time in this next example—but we're going to speed things up a bit. We'll be focusing on our picking hand, switching from palm-muted 16th notes on the low E string to accenting full, six-string chord strums. The first chord sequence is Bm11, which we will immediately start with a hammer-on from the fifth fret to the seventh fret of the low E string with our first and third fingers, respectively. The second chord sequence is G6add9/#4, which will start with a pull-off from the fifth fret to the third fret with our second and first fingers, respectively. Be sure to start at a slower tempo and work your way up to 140 bpm.

EXAMPLE 6

In this example, we'll be playing a riff in 9/8 time and using straight 16th notes throughout. This example will have you working on your alternate picking and string skipping in certain parts. Be sure to get the pattern down on one chord before working through the entire riff. Goal Tempo: 100 bpm.

CHAPTER 7
DROP D TUNING

EXAMPLE 1

In this next example, we're going to switch to Drop D tuning (D–A–D–G–B–E), and play a two-part riff that uses eighth-note triplets. Section A is single-note-based, with several spots that feature muted pick scratches. This will force you to work on how quickly you can go from playing a fretted note to playing a properly muted pick scratch without any excess string noise. Section B is chord based and features the same rhythm throughout. We'll also be frequently changing the notes that we play on the D string for some of these chords. Goal tempo is 150 bpm.

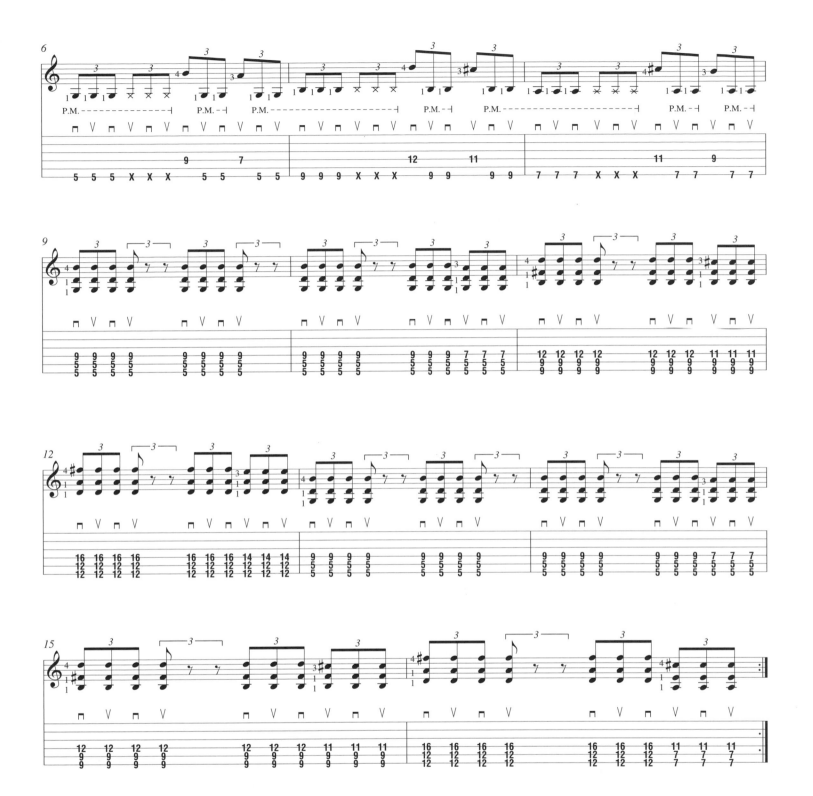

EXAMPLE 2

In this next example, also played in Drop D tuning, we'll explore some ways that you can incorporate open strings when writing riffs in this tuning. We'll start off by playing dotted-eighth-note rhythms on chords that are all based around a Bsus4-type voicing in second position. After that, we'll be moving up the fretboard to play several different chords on the D, G, B, and high E strings. Throughout this series of chords, we'll only be fretting notes on the G and B strings while the open D and high E strings ring out. In every other measure, 16th-note palm mutes of the open sixth string are played, beginning on the second 16th note of beat 4. Goal tempo is 120 bpm.

Drop D tuning:
(low to high) D-A-D-G-B-E

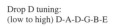

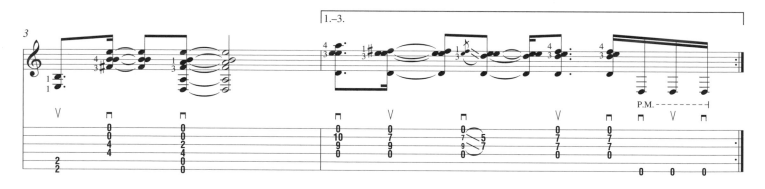

EXAMPLE 3

Here's a two-part riff in Drop D tuning. The A section starts with a three-note chord—essentially, the root, 5th, and 3rd—played on the lower three strings of the guitar (E, A, and D) and in a dotted-eighth-note rhythm. These chord strums are followed by four palm-muted 16th notes on the low E and D strings (notice that they're the same notes, but played in two different octaves). We'll continue this pattern for the second and third measures, using the same rhythm but different chords. The fourth measure starts with the same rhythm but finishes with a quarter-note strum of a Dmaj9 chord. The B section mirrors the chords from the A section but changes the rhythm to a faster-paced feel. Goal tempo is 115 bpm.

EXAMPLE 4

For this next example in Drop D, we're going to take a look at a fast-paced riff that starts with an F#m chord voiced on the fourth and seventh frets. The first two measures have a gallop-style rhythm consisting of an eighth-note strum of the whole chord and two palm-muted 16th notes on the sixth string. For the following two measures, we'll slide this same chord shape to a few different positions on the fretboard to complete the riff. Be sure to really focus on syncing your alternate picking with the 16th notes, as well as your palm-muting control. Goal tempo is 135 bpm.

EXAMPLE 5

For this next example in Drop D tuning, we'll be in 4/4 time, but we'll have a good mix of rhythms throughout the riff, including dotted eighths, straight eighths, 16th notes, and more. The result is a new rhythm in each measure versus a riff that has a repeating theme or rhythm throughout. I would recommend closely examining each measure, one by one, especially the picking, as there are certain parts that you'll accent with a downstroke, and others that you'll accent with an upstroke. There are also sections that will require palm muting, arpeggiation, and letting chords sustain. Goal tempo is 120 bpm.

EXAMPLE 6

Sometimes, creating a pattern of only a few notes out of a given chord or progression is a good way to start a riff. In this case, I created a group of three notes on the lower three strings of the guitar. Then I decided to incorporate some dynamics by slowly building up the pattern, going from palm muting it while lightly picking to opening it up and picking it harder. Next, I transitioned from the original three-note pattern to playing full, six-string chords. Goal Tempo: 130 bpm.

Drop D tuning:
(low to high) D-A-D-G-B-E

♩ = 130

*Gradually release P.M.

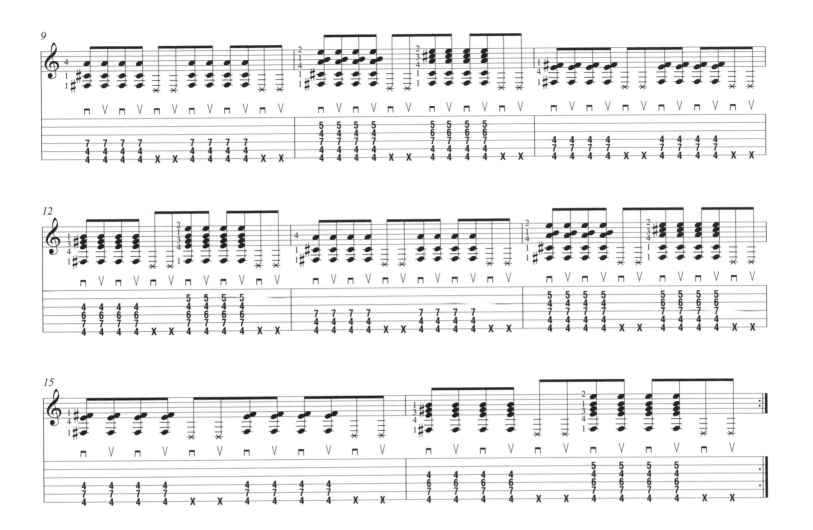

EXAMPLE 7

Here's another riff in Drop D tuning. We'll be playing in 7/4 time and using some non-traditional chord shapes that happen to sound great in a drop tuning, producing a very big, open sound. This riff is also an example of writing something that goes over the bar line and doesn't repeat the same way in the next measure. All of the single notes that are played on the low E string will be palm muted with your picking hand, while each of the chords will be strummed open in order to ring out loudly. Definitely focus on the picking part, as it may take a little while to get a feel for switching between these chords. Goal Tempo: 115 bpm.

Drop D tuning:
(low to high) D-A-D-G-B-E

EXAMPLE 8

In this example, we'll be exploring a couple of things: Drop D tuning and another odd time signature commonly used in progressive rock, 11/8. Writing music in Drop D is very popular in progressive rock these days, and has been for a while. Drop D can really open up your options for certain chord voicings and note choices that would be unreachable in standard tuning. This riff primarily focuses on palm muting and accenting the chords when you hit them open. Goal tempo is 120 bpm.

Drop D tuning:
(low to high) D-A-D-G-B-E

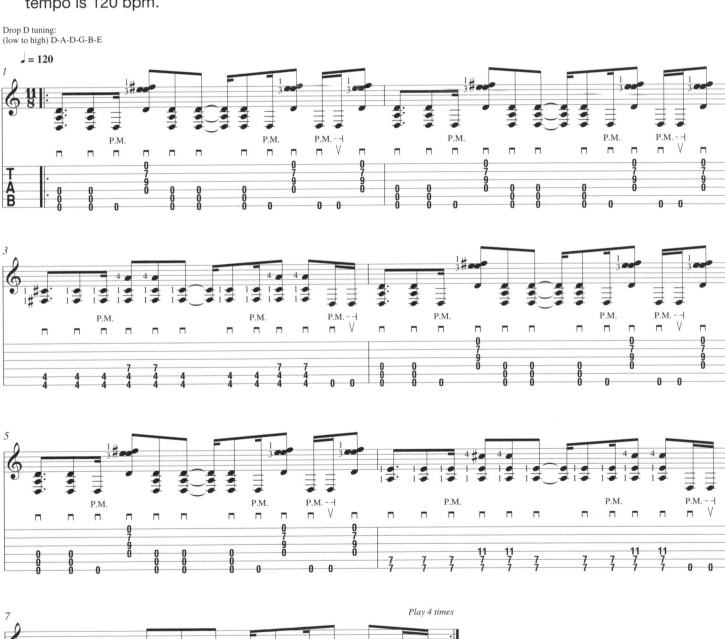

CHAPTER 8
SEVEN-STRING GUITAR

EXAMPLE 1

For this first seven-string example, we'll be in normal 4/4 time. The first measure will start off with four dotted-eighth-note hits on an F#m11 chord, switching between strumming the entire chord and just hitting the root, ♭7th, and ♭3rd. This is followed by a group of four 16th notes on the low E string, starting with a hammer onto the second fret and having the last note ring out into the next measure. The second measure starts with the same chord but will end with a longer 16th-note pattern that incorporates the open low B string. Moving on to the third measure, we'll be playing an Asus2/add#4 chord. We'll keep the same type of feel and rhythm for this section as we alternate between strumming the entire chord and just the bottom three strings. Goal tempo is 110 bpm.

EXAMPLE 2

This next example is in 6/4 and is a good one for easing yourself into incorporating the seventh string of the guitar into your riff playing. We'll be starting each pattern with a couple of dotted-eighth-note strums on the chord that we're holding down on the low E, A, and D strings, Bm. Right after that, we'll move up to the low B string for a five-note gallop pattern consisting of two 16th notes, a single eighth note, and two more 16th notes. Pick this pattern as follows: down-up-down-down-up. Goal tempo is 130 bpm.

EXAMPLE 3

In this next example, we'll be taking a look at how the seven-string guitar can expand your options, harmonically and rhythmically, when writing music. The riff is played in 6/4 time and is mostly single-note-based, with a few spots where we will strum a full chord and let it sustain. We'll be using some hammer-ons and pull-offs, as well as some 16th-note palm mutes on the low B string for an added percussive dynamic. Goal tempo is 120 bpm.

EXAMPLE 4

We'll be playing in a 5/8 time signature in this next seven-string example. This riff is a good example of how you can use the seventh string of your guitar to reach certain notes for chords that you otherwise would not be able to play. Try to let each note of the chord ring out right up until you switch to the next one. Goal Tempo: 120 bpm.

EXAMPLE 5

Oftentimes, people will write a progression by starting with the chords, but another approach is to create a simple single-note melody first or, if you are in a band setting in which there is already a melody in place, you can use that as a starting point and build your chords underneath it. Having a seven-string guitar can also help you create chord voicings that otherwise would be unplayable. This riff is in 6/4 time and incorporates the seventh string for both single notes and for chords. Try practicing the riff with a metronome with the eighth-note accent on. Goal Tempo: 110 bpm.

CHAPTER 9
RIFF CONSTRUCTION

In this chapter, we're going to take an in-depth look at many of the approaches that I use to create new riffs using four of the examples already presented in the book as models. These approaches include using odd note groupings, incorporating open strings into chord voicings for a larger sound, building a progression by adding or changing one note at a time in a chord or riff, drop-tuning chord options, and tastefully incorporating the seventh string into your riffs. The model examples can be found on page 24 for riff 1, page 56 for riff 2, page 64 for riff 3, and page 12 for riff 4.

RIFF 1

RIFF 2

In this example, we'll be in Drop D tuning. Sometimes, creating a pattern of only a few notes out of a given chord or progression is a good way to start a riff. In this case, I created a group of three notes on the lower three strings of the guitar. Then I decided to incorporate some dynamics by slowly building up the pattern, going from palm muting it while lightly picking to opening it up and picking it harder. Next, I transitioned from the original three-note pattern to playing full, six-string chords.

Drop D tuning:
(low to high) D-A-D-G-B-E

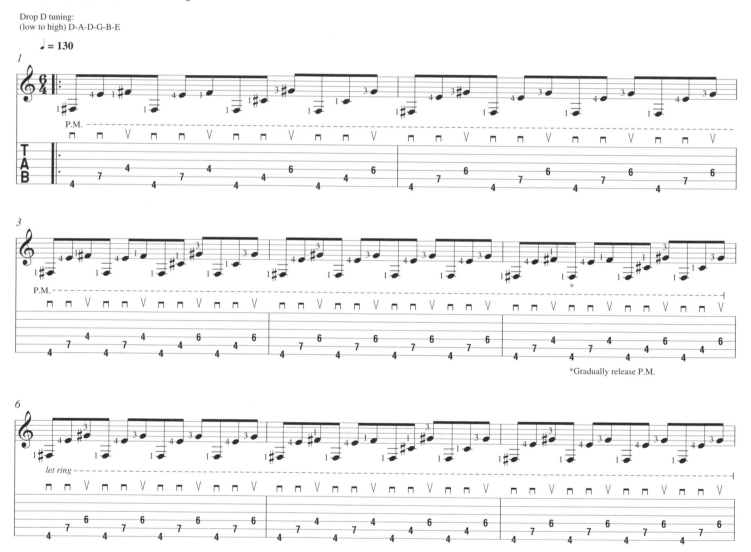

*Gradually release P.M.

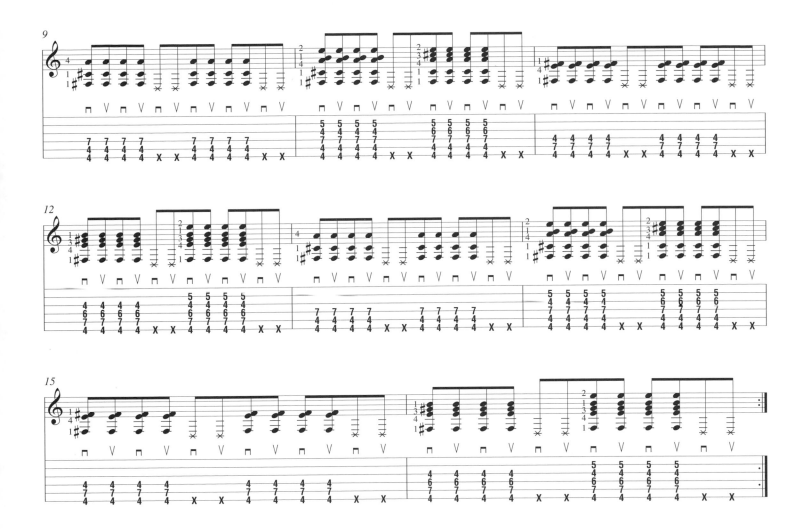

RIFF 3

Oftentimes, people will write a progression by starting with the chords, but another approach is to create a simple single-note melody first or, if you are in a band setting in which there is already a melody in place, you can use that as a starting point and build your chords underneath it. Having a seven-string guitar can also help you create chord voicings that otherwise would be unplayable.

RIFF 4

In this next example, we'll look at some chords in the key of B major and how we can link them together by using single-note gallop patterns, as well as arpeggiating certain parts of the chords to produce a more complete-sounding riff. It starts off with a Badd9 chord, then moves on to Bsus2, Bmaj7, and, finally, G#m7. Practice the chord changes before trying to play the entire sequence. This riff also focuses on pick control, combining both alternate picking and economy (sweep) picking. Goal tempo is 130 bpm.

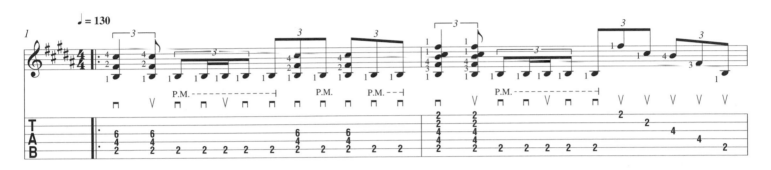

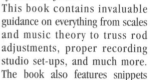

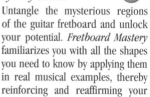

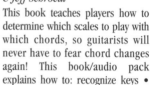

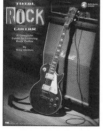

GUITAR *signature licks*

Signature Licks book/audio packs provide a step-by-step breakdown of "right from the record" riffs, licks, and solos so you can jam along with your favorite bands. They contain performance notes and an overview of each artist's or group's style, with note-for-note transcriptions in notes and tab. The CDs or online audio tracks feature full-band demos at both normal and slow speeds.

AC/DC
14041352................$22.99

AEROSMITH 1973-1979
00695106................$22.95

AEROSMITH 1979-1998
00695219................$22.95

DUANE ALLMAN
00696042................$22.99

BEST OF CHET ATKINS
00695752................$22.95

AVENGED SEVENFOLD
00696473................$22.99

BEST OF THE BEATLES FOR ACOUSTIC GUITAR
00695453................$22.99

THE BEATLES BASS
00695283................$22.95

THE BEATLES FAVORITES
00695096................$24.95

THE BEATLES HITS
00695049................$24.95

JEFF BECK
00696427................$22.99

BEST OF GEORGE BENSON
00695418................$22.95

BEST OF BLACK SABBATH
00695249................$22.95

BLUES BREAKERS WITH JOHN MAYALL & ERIC CLAPTON
00696374................$22.99

BON JOVI
00696380................$22.99

ROY BUCHANAN
00696654................$22.99

KENNY BURRELL
00695830................$22.99

BEST OF CHARLIE CHRISTIAN
00695584................$22.95

BEST OF ERIC CLAPTON
00695038................$24.99

ERIC CLAPTON – FROM THE ALBUM UNPLUGGED
00695250................$24.95

BEST OF CREAM
00695251................$22.95

CREEDANCE CLEARWATER REVIVAL
00695924................$22.95

DEEP PURPLE – GREATEST HITS
00695625................$22.99

THE BEST OF DEF LEPPARD
00696516................$22.95

DREAM THEATER
00111943................$24.99

TOMMY EMMANUEL
00696409................$22.99

ESSENTIAL JAZZ GUITAR
00695875................$19.99

FAMOUS ROCK GUITAR SOLOS
00695590................$19.95

FLEETWOOD MAC
00696416................$22.99

BEST OF FOO FIGHTERS
00695481................$24.95

ROBBEN FORD
00695903................$22.95

BEST OF GRANT GREEN
00695747................$22.99

PETER GREEN
00145386................$22.99

THE GUITARS OF ELVIS – 2ND ED.
00174800................$22.99

BEST OF GUNS N' ROSES
00695183................$24.99

THE BEST OF BUDDY GUY
00695186................$22.99

JIM HALL
00695848................$22.99

JIMI HENDRIX
00696560................$24.99

JIMI HENDRIX – VOLUME 2
00695835................$24.95

JOHN LEE HOOKER
00695894................$19.99

BEST OF JAZZ GUITAR
00695586................$24.95

ERIC JOHNSON
00699317................$24.95

ROBERT JOHNSON
00695264................$22.95

BARNEY KESSEL
00696009................$22.99

THE ESSENTIAL ALBERT KING
00695713................$22.95

B.B. KING – BLUES LEGEND
00696039................$22.99

B.B. KING – THE DEFINITIVE COLLECTION
00695635................$22.95

B.B. KING – MASTER BLUESMAN
00699923................$24.99

MARK KNOPFLER
00695178................$22.95

LYNYRD SKYNYRD
00695872................$24.95

THE BEST OF YNGWIE MALMSTEEN
00695669................$22.95

BEST OF PAT MARTINO
00695632................$24.99

MEGADETH
00696421................$22.99

WES MONTGOMERY
00695387................$24.95

BEST OF NIRVANA
00695483................$24.95

VERY BEST OF OZZY OSBOURNE
00695431................$22.95

BRAD PAISLEY
00696379................$22.99

BEST OF JOE PASS
00695730................$22.95

JACO PASTORIUS
00695544................$24.95

TOM PETTY
00696021................$22.99

PINK FLOYD
00103659................$24.99

PINK FLOYD – EARLY CLASSICS
00695566................$22.95

BEST OF QUEEN
00695097................$24.95

RADIOHEAD
00109304................$24.99

BEST OF RAGE AGAINST THE MACHINE
00695480................$24.95

RED HOT CHILI PEPPERS
00695173................$22.95

RED HOT CHILI PEPPERS – GREATEST HITS
00695828................$24.99

BEST OF DJANGO REINHARDT
00695660................$24.95

BEST OF ROCK 'N' ROLL GUITAR
00695559................$19.95

BEST OF ROCKABILLY GUITAR
00695785................$19.95

BEST OF JOE SATRIANI
00695216................$22.95

SLASH
00696576................$22.99

SLAYER
00121281 Guitar................$22.99

THE BEST OF SOUL GUITAR
00695703................$19.95

BEST OF SOUTHERN ROCK
00695560................$19.95

STEELY DAN
00696015................$22.99

MIKE STERN
00695800................$24.99

BEST OF SURF GUITAR
00695822................$19.99

STEVE VAI
00673247................$22.95

STEVE VAI – ALIEN LOVE SECRETS: THE NAKED VAMPS
00695223................$22.95

STEVE VAI – FIRE GARDEN: THE NAKED VAMPS
00695166................$22.95

STEVE VAI – THE ULTRA ZONE: NAKED VAMPS
00695684................$22.95

VAN HALEN
00110227................$24.99

STEVIE RAY VAUGHAN – 2ND ED.
00699316................$24.95

THE GUITAR STYLE OF STEVIE RAY VAUGHAN
00695155................$24.95

BEST OF THE VENTURES
00695772................$19.95

THE WHO – 2ND ED.
00695561................$22.95

JOHNNY WINTER
00695951................$22.99

YES
00113120................$22.99

NEIL YOUNG – GREATEST HITS
00695988................$22.99

BEST OF ZZ TOP
00695738................$24.95

HAL•LEONARD®

www.halleonard.com

COMPLETE DESCRIPTIONS AND SONGLISTS ONLINE!

Prices, contents and availability subject to change without notice.

0317

RECORDED VERSIONS®

The Best Note-For-Note Transcriptions Available

AUTHENTIC TRANSCRIPTIONS WITH NOTES AND TABLATURE

14037551	AC/DC – Backtracks	$32.99
00690178	Alice in Chains – Acoustic	$19.99
00694865	Alice in Chains – Dirt	$19.95
00690958	Duane Allman Guitar Anthology	$24.99
00694932	Allman Brothers Band – Volume 1	$24.95
00694933	Allman Brothers Band – Volume 2	$24.95
00694934	Allman Brothers Band – Volume 3	$24.95
00123558	Arctic Monkeys – AM	$22.99
00690609	Audioslave	$19.95
00690820	Avenged Sevenfold – City of Evil	$24.95
00691065	Avenged Sevenfold – Waking the Fallen	$22.99
00123140	The Avett Brothers Guitar Collection	$22.99
00690503	Beach Boys – Very Best of	$19.99
00690489	Beatles – 1	$24.99
00694832	Beatles – For Acoustic Guitar	$22.99
00691014	Beatles Rock Band	$34.99
00694914	Beatles – Rubber Soul	$22.99
00694863	Beatles – Sgt. Pepper's Lonely Hearts Club Band	$22.99
00110193	Beatles – Tomorrow Never Knows	$22.99
00690110	Beatles – White Album (Book 1)	$19.95
00691043	Jeff Beck – Wired	$19.99
00692385	Chuck Berry	$22.99
00690835	Billy Talent	$19.95
00147787	Best of the Black Crowes	$19.99
00690901	Best of Black Sabbath	$19.95
14042759	Black Sabbath – 13	$19.99
00690831	blink-182 – Greatest Hits	$19.95
00148544	Michael Bloomfield Guitar Anthology	$24.99
00158600	Joe Bonamassa – Blues of Desperation	$22.99
00690913	Boston	$19.95
00690491	David Bowie – Best of	$19.99
00690873	Breaking Benjamin – Phobia	$19.95
00141446	Best of Lenny Breau	$19.99
00690451	Jeff Buckley – Collection	$24.95
00690957	Bullet for My Valentine – Scream Aim Fire	$22.99
00691159	The Cars – Complete Greatest Hits	$22.99
00691079	Best of Johnny Cash	$22.99
00690590	Eric Clapton – Anthology	$29.95
00690415	Clapton Chronicles – Best of Eric Clapton	$18.95
00690936	Eric Clapton – Complete Clapton	$29.99
00192383	Eric Clapton – I Still Do*	$19.99
00694869	Eric Clapton – Unplugged	$22.95
00138731	Eric Clapton & Friends – The Breeze	$22.99
00690162	The Clash – Best of	$19.95
00101916	Eric Church – Chief	$22.99
00690828	Coheed & Cambria – Good Apollo I'm Burning Star, IV, Vol. 1: From Fear Through the Eyes of Madness	$19.95
00141704	Jesse Cook – Works Vol. 1	$19.99
00127184	Best of Robert Cray	$19.99
00690819	Creedence Clearwater Revival – Best of	$22.95
00690648	The Very Best of Jim Croce	$19.99
00690613	Crosby, Stills & Nash – Best of	$22.95
00691171	Cry of Love – Brother	$22.99
00690967	Death Cab for Cutie – Narrow Stairs	$22.99
00690289	Deep Purple – Best of	$19.99
00690784	Def Leppard – Best of	$22.99
00692240	Bo Diddley	$19.99
00122443	Dream Theater	$24.99
14041903	Bob Dylan for Guitar Tab	$19.99
00139220	Tommy Emmanuel – Little by Little	$24.99
00691186	Evanescence	$22.99
00691181	Five Finger Death Punch – American Capitalist	$22.99
00690664	Fleetwood Mac – Best of	$19.95
00690870	Flyleaf	$19.95
00691115	Foo Fighters – Wasting Light	$22.99
00690805	Robben Ford – Best of	$22.99
00120220	Robben Ford – Guitar Anthology	$24.99
00694920	Free – Best of	$19.95

00691190	Best of Peter Green	$19.99
00113073	Green Day – ¡Uno!	$21.99
00116846	Green Day – ¡Dos!	$21.99
00118259	Green Day – ¡Tré!	$21.99
00212480	Green Day – Revolutionary Radio*	$19.99
00694854	Buddy Guy – Damn Right, I've Got the Blues	$19.95
00690840	Ben Harper – Both Sides of the Gun	$19.95
00694798	George Harrison – Anthology	$19.95
00690841	Scott Henderson – Blues Guitar Collection	$19.95
00692930	Jimi Hendrix – Are You Experienced?	$24.95
00692931	Jimi Hendrix – Axis: Bold As Love	$22.95
00692932	Jimi Hendrix – Electric Ladyland	$24.95
00690017	Jimi Hendrix – Live at Woodstock	$24.95
00690602	Jimi Hendrix – Smash Hits	$24.99
00119619	Jimi Hendrix – People, Hell and Angels	$22.99
00691152	West Coast Seattle Boy: The Jimi Hendrix Anthology	$29.99
00691332	Jimi Hendrix – Winterland (Highlights)	$22.99
00690793	John Lee Hooker Anthology	$24.99
00121961	Imagine Dragons – Night Visions	$22.99
00690688	Incubus – A Crow Left of the Murder	$19.95
00690790	Iron Maiden Anthology	$24.99
00690684	Jethro Tull – Aqualung	$19.95
00690814	John5 – Songs for Sanity	$19.95
00690751	John5 – Vertigo	$19.95
00122439	Jack Johnson – From Here to Now to You	$22.99
00690271	Robert Johnson – New Transcriptions	$24.99
00699131	Janis Joplin – Best of	$19.95
00690427	Judas Priest – Best of	$22.99
00120814	Killswitch Engage – Disarm the Descent	$22.99
00124869	Albert King with Stevie Ray Vaughan – In Session	$22.99
00694903	Kiss – Best of	$24.95
00690355	Kiss – Destroyer	$16.95
00690834	Lamb of God – Ashes of the Wake	$19.95
00690875	Lamb of God – Sacrament	$19.95
00114563	The Lumineers	$22.99
00690955	Lynyrd Skynyrd – All-Time Greatest Hits	$22.99
00694954	Lynyrd Skynyrd – New Best of	$19.95
00690754	Marilyn Manson – Lest We Forget	$19.95
00694956	Bob Marley– Legend	$19.95
00694945	Bob Marley– Songs of Freedom	$24.95
00139168	Pat Martino – Guitar Anthology	$24.99
00129105	John McLaughlin Guitar Tab Anthology	$24.99
00120080	Don McLean – Songbook	$19.95
00694951	Megadeth – Rust in Peace	$22.95
00691185	Megadeth – Th1rt3en	$22.99
00690505	John Mellencamp – Guitar Collection	$19.95
00209876	Metallica – Hardwired...To Self-Destruct	$22.99
00690646	Pat Metheny – One Quiet Night	$19.95
00690558	Pat Metheny – Trio: 99>00	$24.99
00118836	Pat Metheny – Unity Band	$22.99
00690040	Steve Miller Band – Young Hearts	$19.95
00119338	Ministry Guitar Tab Collection	$24.99
00102591	Wes Montgomery Guitar Anthology	$24.99
00691070	Mumford & Sons – Sigh No More	$22.99
00151195	Muse – Drones	$19.99
00694883	Nirvana – Nevermind	$19.95
00690026	Nirvana – Unplugged in New York	$19.95
00690807	The Offspring – Greatest Hits	$19.95
00694847	Ozzy Osbourne – Best of	$22.95
00690933	Best of Brad Paisley	$22.95
00690995	Brad Paisley – Play: The Guitar Album	$24.99
00694855	Pearl Jam – Ten	$22.99
00690439	A Perfect Circle – Mer De Noms	$19.95
00690499	Tom Petty – Definitive Guitar Collection	$19.99
00121933	Pink Floyd – Acoustic Guitar Collection	$22.99
00690428	Pink Floyd – Dark Side of the Moon	$19.95
00690789	Poison – Best of	$19.95
00694975	Queen – Greatest Hits	$24.95
00690670	Queensryche – Very Best of	$22.99
00109303	Radiohead Guitar Anthology	$24.99
00694910	Rage Against the Machine	$19.95
00119834	Rage Against the Machine – Guitar Anthology	$22.99

00690055	Red Hot Chili Peppers – Blood Sugar Sex Magik	$19.95
00690584	Red Hot Chili Peppers – By the Way	$19.95
00209876	Red Hot Chili Peppers – The Getaway	$22.99
00691166	Red Hot Chili Peppers – I'm with You	$22.99
00690852	Red Hot Chili Peppers –Stadium Arcadium	$24.95
00690511	Django Reinhardt – Definitive Collection	$22.99
14043417	Rodrigo y Gabriela – 9 Dead Alive	$19.99
00690631	Rolling Stones – Guitar Anthology	$27.95
00694976	Rolling Stones – Some Girls	$22.95
00690264	The Rolling Stones – Tattoo You	$19.95
00690685	David Lee Roth – Eat 'Em and Smile	$19.95
00690942	David Lee Roth and the Songs of Van Halen	$19.95
00151826	Royal Blood	$22.99
00174797	Santana – IV*	$22.99
00690031	Santana's Greatest Hits	$19.95
00128870	Matt Schofield Guitar Tab Collection	$22.99
00690566	Scorpions – Best of	$22.95
00690604	Bob Seger – Guitar Collection	$22.99
00138870	Ed Sheeran – X	$19.99
00690803	Kenny Wayne Shepherd Band – Best of	$19.95
00151178	Kenny Wayne Shepherd – Ledbetter Heights (20th Anniversary Edition)	$19.99
00122218	Skillet – Rise	$22.99
00691114	Slash – Guitar Anthology	$24.99
00690813	Slayer – Guitar Collection	$19.99
00120004	Steely Dan – Best of	$24.95
00694921	Steppenwolf – Best of	$22.95
00690655	Mike Stern – Best of	$22.99
00690520	Styx Guitar Collection	$19.95
00120081	Sublime	$19.99
00120122	Sublime – 40oz. to Freedom	$19.95
00690767	Switchfoot – The Beautiful Letdown	$19.95
00690993	Taylor Swift – Fearless	$22.99
00142151	Taylor Swift – 1989	$22.99
00115957	Taylor Swift – Red	$21.99
00690531	System of a Down – Toxicity	$19.95
00694824	James Taylor – Best of	$19.99
00150209	Trans-Siberian Orchestra Guitar Anthology	$19.99
00123862	Trivium – Vengeance Falls	$22.99
00690683	Robin Trower – Bridge of Sighs	$19.95
00660137	Steve Vai – Passion & Warfare	$24.95
00110385	Steve Vai – The Story of Light	$22.99
00690116	Stevie Ray Vaughan – Guitar Collection	$24.95
00660058	Stevie Ray Vaughan – Lightnin' Blues 1983-1987	$27.99
00694835	Stevie Ray Vaughan – The Sky Is Crying	$22.95
00690015	Stevie Ray Vaughan – Texas Flood	$19.99
00183213	Volbeat – Seal the Deal & Let's Boogie*	$19.99
00152161	Doc Watson – Guitar Anthology	$22.99
00690071	Weezer (The Blue Album)	$19.95
00690966	Weezer – (Red Album)	$19.99
00172118	Weezer – (The White Album)*	$19.99
00691941	The Who – Acoustic Guitar Collection	$22.99
00690447	The Who – Best of	$24.95
00122303	Yes Guitar Collection	$22.99
00690916	The Best of Dwight Yoakam	$19.95
00691020	Neil Young – After the Gold Rush	$22.99
00691019	Neil Young – Everybody Knows This Is Nowhere	$19.99
00691021	Neil Young – Harvest Moon	$22.99
00690905	Neil Young – Rust Never Sleeps	$19.99
00690623	Frank Zappa – Over-Nite Sensation	$22.99
00121684	ZZ Top – Early Classics	$24.99
00690589	ZZ Top Guitar Anthology	$24.95

COMPLETE SERIES LIST ONLINE!

HAL•LEONARD®
www.halleonard.com

Prices and availability subject to change without notice.
*Tab transcriptions only.

0617